TAMSIN
AND THE DARK

KEEP OUT

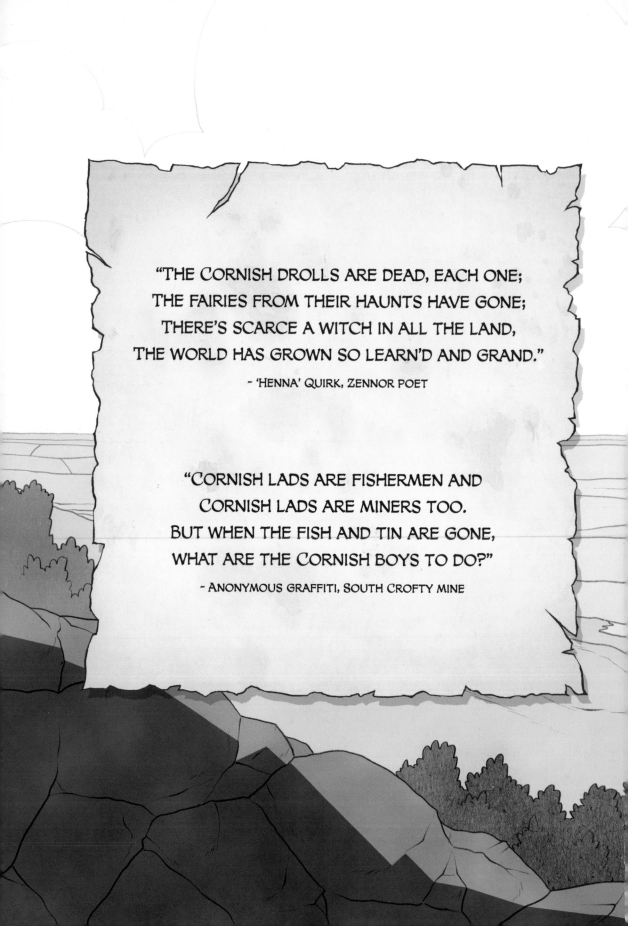

"THE CORNISH DROLLS ARE DEAD, EACH ONE;
THE FAIRIES FROM THEIR HAUNTS HAVE GONE;
THERE'S SCARCE A WITCH IN ALL THE LAND,
THE WORLD HAS GROWN SO LEARN'D AND GRAND."
~ 'HENNA' QUIRK, ZENNOR POET

"CORNISH LADS ARE FISHERMEN AND
CORNISH LADS ARE MINERS TOO.
BUT WHEN THE FISH AND TIN ARE GONE,
WHAT ARE THE CORNISH BOYS TO DO?"
~ ANONYMOUS GRAFFITI, SOUTH CROFTY MINE

chapter ONE

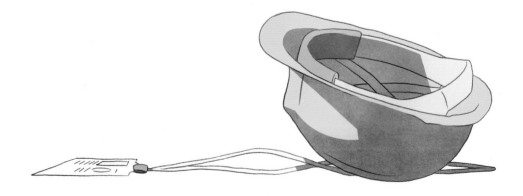

TAMSIN AND THE DARK

BY NEILL CAMERON AND KATE BROWN

Tamsin and the Dark
is a
DAVID FICKLING BOOK

First published in Great Britain in 2018 by
David Fickling Books,
31 Beaumont Street,
Oxford, OX1 2NP
www.davidficklingbooks.com

Text © Neill Cameron, 2018
Illustrations © Kate Brown, 2018

978-1-910989-95-1

1 3 5 7 9 10 8 6 4 2

Papers used by David Fickling Books are from well-managed forests
and other responsible sources.

DAVID FICKLING BOOKS Reg. No. 8340307

A CIP catalogue record for this book is available from the British
Library.

Printed and bound in Great Britain by Sterling.

ANYWAY, LOOKS LIKE YOU'RE GETTING THE HANG OF IT.

I... KIND OF. YOU JUST HAVE TO... THINK ABOUT WHAT YOU WANT IT TO DO. YOU HAVE TO THINK **REALLY HARD.**

THAT'S IT. PSYCHIC OPERATING INTERFACE, SEE? YOU FORM A THOUGHT, AND THEN WILL IT INTO THE WORLD.

YOU CAN MANAGE A LOT WORKING ON INSTINCT, LIKE YOUR LITTLE LIGHT-TRICK, THERE.

BUT THE MORE YOU PRACTISE, THE MORE COMPLEX THOUGHT-FORMS YOU CAN SHAPE, THE MORE YOU'LL BE ABLE TO DO WITH IT.

AARGH. I DON'T **GET** THIS STUFF. I DON'T **GET** IT!

WELL, YOU'RE GOING TO HAVE TO TRY AND LEARN. YOU'RE THE **LAST PELLAR,** THIS STUFF'S YOUR JOB NOW.

YOU NEED TO KNOW ABOUT SPRIGGANS AND GIANTS, AND PISKEYS AND CHANGELINGS—

YOU **COULD** HELP, YOU KNOW. TELL ME WHAT I HAVE TO DO.

WELL, THAT'S THE THING. I CAME TO TELL YOU, I WON'T BE AROUND FOR A WHILE. GOT A BIT OF BUSINESS TO TAKE CARE OF UP NORTH.

WHAT "BUSINESS"? YOU ARE A BIRD.

I KEEP TELLING YOU, LOVE. IRONS IN A LOT OF FIRES, INNIT?

RIGHT. BECAUSE YOU ARE KING ARTHUR.

THAT'S RIGHT. BE SEEING YOU.

WELL, **THANK** YOU, YOU **LOVELY** BIRD!

MATE. **LOOK** AT THE STATE OF THAT.

AND THIS WAS WHAT IT WAS ALL FOR. THE REASON ALL THIS IS HERE — THE **CASSITERITE**, THE TIN ORE.

IT'S A FASCINATING MINERAL. THIS AREA IN PARTICULAR IS KNOWN FOR ITS PSEUDOMORPHS, WHERE THE TIN ACTUALLY REPLACES AND TAKES ON THE SHAPE OF ANOTHER MINERAL.

THE TERM PSEUDOMORPH LITERALLY MEANS FALSE FORM; THERE ARE TWO TYPES: INFILTRATION AND SUBSTITUTION, AND...

...CAN'T BELIEVE SHE HAD THE NERVE TO COME BACK.

BET YOU SHE'S KNOCKED UP AGAIN BY CHRISTMAS...

HEY! ARE YOU TALKING ABOUT MY SISTER? CAUSE I'LL GIVE YOU SOMETHING TO TALK ABOUT!

BLAKE TRESCOTHICK!

MISTER PENVOSE HAS **VERY GENEROUSLY** COME FROM THE MINE PRESERVATION TRUST TO SHARE HIS TIME AND EXPERTISE WITH US.

YOU COULD AT **LEAST** HAVE THE DECENCY TO LISTEN...!

WHATEVER. IT'S BORING. IT'S JUST **ROCKS**.

THESE **ROCKS** ARE YOUR HERITAGE, BOY, YOUR HISTORY.

THAT'S **IT**. IT'S HISTORY. IT'S ALL DEAD AND GONE. YOUR DUMB MINES ARE ALL CLOSED, AND NOBODY CARES. IT'S **POINTLESS**.

YOU CAN GO AND STAND AT THE ENTRANCE, BLAKE. AND EXPECT DETENTION WHEN WE GET BACK TO SCHOOL.

WHATEVER. WHAT DO I CARE?

...WHAT ARE YOU STARING AT, STICK WEIRDO?

!

...

23

WHOA.

THERE YOU GO, THE OLD CODGER'LL BE HAPPY. THE MINE'S OPEN AGAIN!

MAN, I WONDER HOW FAR DOWN IT GOES.

GO AND HAVE A LOOK.

WHAT?

GO ON, CLIMB DOWN A BIT, I DARE YOU.

YOU CLIMB DOWN.

I DARED YOU FIRST. WHAT'S THE MATTER, YOU SCARED OF THE DARK?

HE IS! SINCE HE WAS A KID! WHENEVER WE HAD SLEEPOVERS, HE ALWAYS HAD TO HAVE THE LIGHT ON!

SHUT UP, KYLE!

MAYBE WE SHOULD GO AND ASK YOUR LITTLE SISTER. SHE SEEMS PRETTY BRAVE.

...

HAHA! THAT'S RIGHT, GO DOWN UNTIL WE CAN'T SEE YOU!

UM...

FINE. WHATEVER. NO PROBLEM.

Danger! Disused M... ...aft

MORGAN, BE CAREFUL.

...

...NUTS TO THIS, I'M GOING BACK UP.

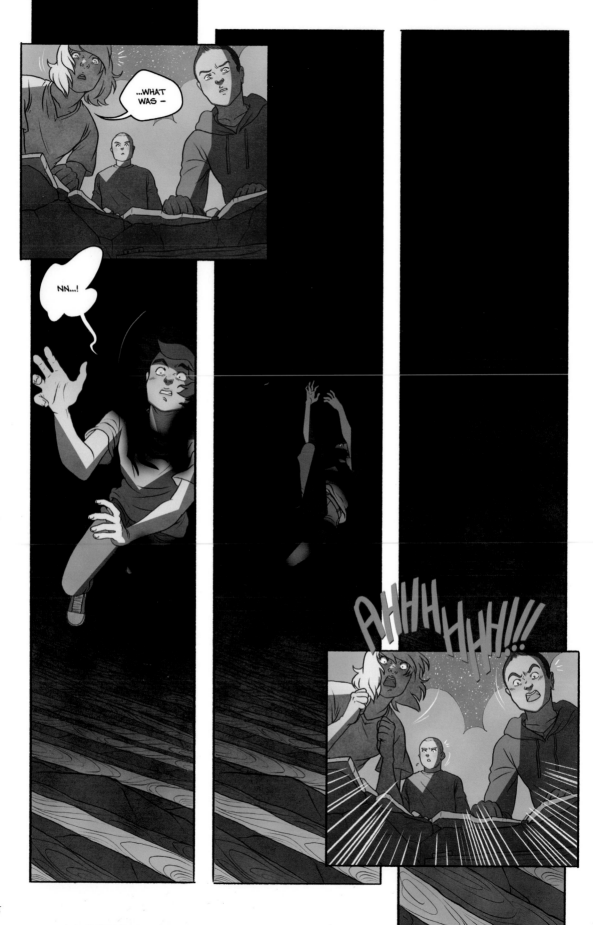

TRAVIS? KYLE?

WHAT ARE YOU GUYS DOING HERE? WHERE'S MORGAN?

WE WERE UP AT THE OLD ENGINE HOUSE, MESSING AROUND...

WE DIDN'T MEAN ANY HARM, BUT BLAKE DARED HIM AND THEN SOMETHING HAPPENED AND...

WHERE'S MORGAN?

IN THE TIME BEFORE TIME, IN THE NORTH, THERE WAS AN ISLAND.

A BITTER, BLASTED, WIND-RAVAGED PLACE, ALONE IN A VAST SEA.

AND TO THIS HAUNTED ISLE THERE CAME MEN AND WOMEN, SURVIVORS OF A GREAT WAR. LOOKING, AT THE ENDS OF THE WORLD, FOR A PLACE TO MAKE THEIR HOME.

BUT THE ISLAND, BLEAK THOUGH IT WAS, WAS NOT FREE OF DENIZENS.

A RACE OF **GIANTS** DWELT THERE. MONSTROUS IN THEIR STRENGTH AND TERRIBLE IN THEIR CRUELTY.

BUT THE PEOPLE'S NEED WAS GREAT, AND IT GAVE TO THEM A DESPERATE STRENGTH.

AND SO, THERE WAS **WAR**.

34

chapter two

12th April

Dear Diary, Today was cool
I guess. Found a weird shadow
monster. Blasted it.

WRR...

TH WRR...

THE WAR WAS ENDED, WITH THE DEATH OF THE GIANT GOGMAGOG.

BUT HATRED SO POWERFUL COULD NOT BE VANQUISHED FOREVER.

IT SLEPT. IN THE GROUND, IN THE DEEP.

IN THE DARK.

AND FROM TIME TO TIME IT WOULD FIND WAYS TO CREEP OUT...

MAN AND GIANT WOULD SLAY ONE ANOTHER ONCE MORE.

AND THE WORLD WOULD AGAIN KNOW DEATH, AND FEAR, AND CHAOS.

UNTIL THE LAST LIVING GIANT—THE GAUNT ONE—SAW THAT THIS COULD NOT CONTINUE, AND DARED TO DREAM OF A NEW WORLD.

A WORLD OF PEACE.

AND SO A BARGAIN WAS STRUCK, AND THE LAND WAS HANDED TO THE PEOPLE.

TO BE WORKED, TO BE TENDED.

TO BE THEIR OWN, AS LONG AS THEY REMEMBERED. AND AS LONG AS THEY PAID **THE TRIBUTE.**

AND SO, THE LAST GIANT IN CORNWALL WENT TO SLEEP. TO HOLD BACK THE DARK, WITH HIS DREAMS.

AND BY THE STRENGTH OF THE ARRANGEMENT, IT WAS HELD BACK.

HELD BACK, BUT NEVER **GONE.** THE DARK WAS ALWAYS THERE, UNDER THE EARTH. ALWAYS WAITING FOR ITS MOMENT.

ALWAYS SEARCHING FOR A WAY...

AAAH!

...MORGAN?

39

THE ONES THAT TOOK ME. THEY'RE **UP** TO SOMETHING DOWN THERE.

ALL THE PLACES LEFT OVER AND ABANDONED, THE EMPTY MINES. THEY'RE TAKING OVER.

AND THEY WANT TO WIPE US OUT, SO THEY CAN TAKE OVER UP HERE TOO.

HOW DO YOU KNOW ALL THIS?

I DON'T KNOW. I DON'T KNOW WHAT THEY DID...

BUT SOMEHOW, WHEN THEY TOOK ME, THEY DID SOMETHING.

AND I THINK MAYBE NOW YOUR **SIGHT** — YOUR PELLAR GIFT...

I THINK NOW I'VE GOT IT TOO.

WHAT? MORGAN, I DON'T THINK...

YOUR DREAMS, TAMSIN. WITH THE MONSTERS, AND THE DARKNESS...

THERE WAS A SYMBOL IN THEM, RIGHT?

LIKE, A CELTIC-LOOKING KNOT THING...

UM, YEAH.

HOW DID YOU KNOW THAT?

I'VE BEEN HAVING THE **SAME** DREAMS...

EXCUSE ME, HAVE YOU GOT ANY BOOKS ON, UM, SPRIGGANS?

"SPRIGGANS"? HOW DO YOU SPELL THAT?

I... DON'T ACTUALLY KNOW.

WHAT ABOUT FAIRIES? DO YOU HAVE ANY BOOKS ABOUT THEM?

OH! OF COURSE, SWEETIE. OVER IN THE CHILDREN'S SECTION, THERE.

TAMSIN?

...

SHARON!

I BROUGHT TIERNAN ALONG FOR STORY TIME, BUT APPARENTLY THE WOMAN WHO DOES IT IS ILL.

YOU DOING HOMEWORK?

NO, I WAS... LOOKING FOR BOOKS ABOUT FAIRIES.

OR PISKEYS, OR SPRIGGANS OR UNDINES OR KNOCKERS OR...

OH, THEM.

I KNOW ALL ABOUT THEM!

YOUR NAN... DID SHE EVER TELL YOU ABOUT ANYTHING THAT LIVED IN THE MINES?

ABOUT MONSTERS?

OH, SURE. THE BUCCAS?

"BUCCAS"?

THE SMALL FOLK, WHO LIVE DOWN THE MINES. BUT THEY'RE NOT MONSTERS. MOSTLY, IN THE STORIES, THEY'RE FRIENDLY.

THERE'S LOTS ABOUT THEM HELPING MINERS – AVOIDING CAVE-INS, OR LEADING THEM TO A GOOD LODE OR WHATEVER.

I HEARD ONE WHERE THEY'RE ACTUALLY THE SPIRITS OF DEAD MINERS. LIKE, HELPING THEIR FRIENDS.

THAT DOESN'T SOUND RIGHT.

THEY'RE NOT... ANGRY? SCARY?

I MEAN, THERE'S STORIES WHERE, LIKE, THEY TURN NASTY WHEN SOMEONE TRIES TO WELCH ON A DEAL.

BUT THEY'RE NOT MONSTERS.

MAMM-WYNN TOLD ME HOW, EVEN TO THE END, SOME OF THE MINERS'D MAKE THEM AN OFFERING.

A LITTLE PORTION OF THE TIN THEY FOUND THAT DAY. OR EVEN, LIKE, THE END OF THEIR PASTIES.

THEY'D LEAVE IT IN A DARK CORNER OF THE MINE, AND THE NEXT MORNING IT'D BE GONE.

...HOW COME YOU'RE SUDDENLY INTERESTED IN ALL THIS?

I KNOW YOU AND MORGAN HAVE ALWAYS BEEN VERY CLOSE. BUT YOU'VE ALWAYS BEEN VERY DIFFERENT, AS WELL.

I STILL REMEMBER WHEN I REALLY REALISED IT. IT WAS A COUPLE OF YEARS AFTER... AFTER WE LOST YOUR DAD.

MORGAN WAS HAVING TROUBLE SLEEPING. I HAD TO STAY WITH HIM, EVERY NIGHT.

HE'D FINALLY DROP OFF, AND I WOULD COME TO CHECK ON YOU. AND THERE YOU WERE.

ALL THE LIGHTS IN YOUR ROOM OFF. STANDING AT YOUR WINDOW, STARING OUT INTO THE DARK.

YEAH, WELL.

I COULD SEE WHAT WAS OUT THERE.

HEY!

RUSTLE!!!

AAAAAAHHH!!!!

ALL RIGHT — FIRST, WE ARE GOING TO CALL THE POLICE.

TAMSIN, RUN AND FETCH MY BAG — WE'LL STAY HERE AND CHECK ALL THE ROOMS, THE CUPBOARDS, THE DRAWERS, EVERYTHING. OKAY?

Y-YES, MUM!

OH MY GOD OH MY GOD OH MY GOD...

MORGAN! WE HAVE TO HELP! IT'S BABY TIERNAN! SOMEONE—

I KNOW.

I SAW IT, TAMSIN. I SAW WHO TOOK HIM.

IT WAS THEM.

THE CREATURES UNDER THE GROUND.

THE MONSTERS!

49

ARE YOU SURE? IT LOOKS EMPTY. HOW ARE WE GOING TO...

KRESH!!!

WHAT ARE YOU DOING?! SOMEONE LIVES THERE!

THEY DON'T, THOUGH. THAT'S THE POINT.

PEOPLE USED TO LIVE HERE. FISHERMEN AND THEIR SONS. BUT ONE BY ONE, ALL THE HOUSES GOT BOUGHT UP BY... RICH BANKERS FROM SURREY.

THEY COME HERE FOR TWO WEEKS IN THE SUMMER. AND THE REST OF THE YEAR IT'S JUST EMPTY.

UNCARED-FOR. DESERTED.

DARK.

AND THEY'VE BEEN BUSY, IN THE DARK.

COME ON. WE HAVE TO GO AFTER THEM...

SURE, BUT...

...DIDN'T YOU USED TO BE AFRAID OF THE DARK?

TAMSIN. CONCENTRATE. THE BUCCAS, REMEMBER?

YOU'RE GOING TO HAVE TO FIGHT THEM. TO SAVE BABY TIERNAN.

DON'T WORRY ABOUT THOSE GUYS.

SCRAWNY LITTLE GOLLUM-LOOKING WEIRDOS.

THEY GOT THE DROP ON ME LAST TIME, BUT NOW I'M READY.

I THINK I CAN HANDLE A FEW...

58

GOO.

COUGH

TAMSIN...?

SNFF

THAT THING.

I LOST LUCKY STICK.

I LOST.

RRRRUMBLE!!!

SPLASH!!!

AT LAST, WE HAVE IT.

AT LAST, WE CAN WAKE HIM.

AND HE WILL WIPE HUMANITY FROM THIS WORLD!

chapter three

YOU...

YOU'RE A BUCCA, AREN'T YOU? ONE OF THE SMALL FOLK.

YOU SAVED MY BABY?

BUCCAS JUST TRY TO HELP!

SPRIGGANS TAKE THE CHILD! SPRIGGANS!

THE GHOST-GIANTS! THE DEVILS IN THE DARK!

IT'S ALL TRUE...

I...

SHARON! THIS IS CRAZY! YOU'RE ALL CRAZY!

DO YOU... DO YOU HAVE A NAME?

BUCCA...

BUCCA'S NAME IS SALLY.

THANK YOU, SALLY.

SHE LOOKED AFTER ME! THE WHOLE TIME I WAS TRAPPED DOWN THERE, SHE SNUCK ME FOOD AND STUFF.

BUCCAS ALWAYS HELP THE PEOPLE!

I HEAR YOU.

WHO ARE YOU?

WE ARE...

SONS OF CORIN. KERNOWYN. CORNISHMEN.

WE WORKED DOWN HERE.

WE DIED DOWN HERE.

AND SINCE MAN FIRST CAME HERE, WE KEPT THE BARGAIN.

NOW, YOU MUST GO.

GO WHERE?

INTO THE DARK...

I... I'M SCARED.

YOU ARE NOT ALONE, CORNISHMAN.

DOWN HERE, YOUR FATHERS WALK WITH YOU.

OKAY.

84

I WAS HAVING THE MOST WONDERFUL DREAM...

TAMSIN!

YOU DID IT!

WE DID IT.

RIGHT?

MORGAN'S LITTLE SISTER...

TAMSIN. THAT WAS...

THAT WAS THE GREATEST THING I HAVE EVER SEEN IN MY LIFE!

YOU SURFED A HILL! YOU PUNCHED OUT A GHOST GIANT!

ARE YOU A WIZARD?!

AND CAN I BE YOUR APPRENTICE?!!

OH, WELL.

THERE GOES YOUR SECRET IDENTITY.

THERE, THERE.

THAT'S MAYBE ENOUGH EXCITEMENT FOR ONE DAY.

COME ON, LET'S GET BACK. MUM MUST BE GOING SPARE.

The West Briton

Freak Earthquake Rocks Redruth, Camborne

COR, THEY'LL PRINT ANY OLD RUBBISH, WON'T THEY?

AAAH!

WHERE DID YOU COME FROM?

THE SKY.

I'M A BIRD, INNIT?

ANYTHING ABOUT YOU IN THAT PAPER?

WHAT? NO. NO, EVERYONE JUST THINKS IT WAS AN EARTHQUAKE.

THERE'S NOTHING ABOUT ME, OR MORGAN, OR SPRIGGANS OR BUCCAS OR...

AND WHERE HAVE YOU BEEN?

WHO, ME?

I'VE TOLD YOU – I'M KING ARTHUR, INNIT?

PURVIEW.

I EN'T JUST GOT CORNWALL TO WORRY ABOUT. THE WHOLE OF BRITAIN FALLS WITHIN MY, WHATCHAMACALLIT.

BEEN UP IN LEICESTER, AS IT HAPPENS. THE SHADE OF RICHARD III WOKE UP IN A RIGHT HUMP, GOT IN A BARNEY WITH A COUPLE OF LOCAL NAGAS.

COR, THE MESS.

WHAT ARE YOU **TALKING** ABOUT?

YOU SHOULD HAVE BEEN **HERE**!

THERE WERE **EVIL GHOST GIANTS** AND MORGAN WAS A **CHANGELING** AND...

IT WAS HORRIBLE! I NEEDED **HELP**!

SEEMS TO ME YOU'VE **GOT** HELP.

WELL... YEAH.

MORGAN FORCED BLAKE TO SIGN UP WITH HIM TO HELP OUT AT THE MINING PRESERVATION PLACE.

THAT WAY THEY CAN KEEP AN EYE ON THINGS... DOWN THERE.

AND THEY'RE GOING TO, Y'KNOW, HELP ME OUT.

BACK ME UP, AND STUFF.

GOOD. I DUNNO WHERE YOU GOT THIS IDEA YOU HAD TO DO EVERYTHING YOURSELF.

"SECRET IDENTITIES" AND SUCH. HONESTLY.

BEEN READING TOO MANY COMICS.

YOU GOT FRIENDS THERE. YOU'RE PART OF A COMMUNITY. YOU HAVE TO LEAD THEM.

HEH.

RIGHT LITTLE ARMY SHE'S GOT FOR HERSELF THERE, INNIT?

YES.

SHE'S GOING TO NEED IT. YOU KNOW WHAT'S COMING.

YEAH.

YEAH, GOD HELP HER.

I DO.

TO BE CONTINUED

READ TAMSIN'S FIRST ADVENTURE, PLUS OTHER AMAZING BOOKS IN THE PHOENIX PRESENTS SERIES

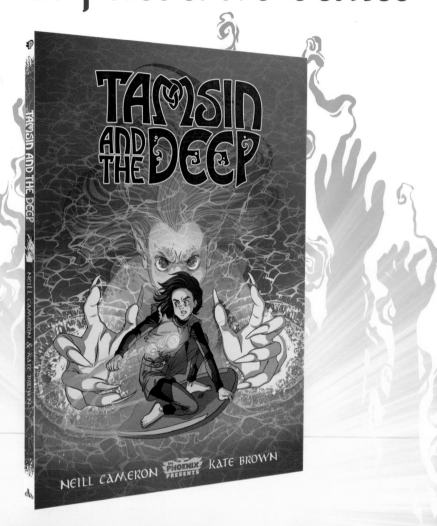